hide
this
french
book

APA Publications (UK) Ltd.
New York London Singapore

hide
this
french
book

Contacting the Editors
Every effort has been made to provide accurate information in this publication, but changes are inevitable. The publisher cannot be responsible for any resulting loss, inconvenience or injury. We would appreciate it if readers would call our attention to any errors or outdated information. We also welcome your suggestions; if you come across a relevant expression not in our phrase book, please contact us: language@apaguide.co.uk

2nd Edition: March 2013
Printed in China by CTPS

Head of Language: Kate Drynan
Writer: Eve-Alice Roustang-Stoller
Design: Bev Speight
Production Manager: Vicky Glover
Illustrator: Kyle Webster

inside

the initiation

Admittance to French culture requires more than just knowing a handful of expressions. If you really wanna get in, you've gotta know slang, street speak, and swear words. Hide This French Book has what it takes so you can talk the talk. No grammar lessons, verb conjugations, or any rules here — just the language that's actually spoken in France today — from the most intimate encounters (and, yeah, we're talking sex) to technology know-how (e-mail, IM, text messaging, Facebook, Twitter).

Stuff you gotta know

It's assumed you already know a little bit of the French language. Most of the expressions provided can be applied to both guys and girls. You'll see if the word or phrase can be applied to ♂**guys** alone and when it's for ♀**girls** only.

We regularly talk about "verlan" or slang. This is where the order of the letters of French words have been mixed up to create a new slang word, you'll soon pick them up! For more on this, see p.9. In case you're uncertain about how to pronounce something in the book and don't want to sound like a fool, go online and download the audio content:
www.insightguides.com/hidethis

Watch out for...

We've labeled the hottest language with **Hot Spots**, so you can easily gauge just how "bad" the expression really is. You'll see:

 These are pretty crude and crass —use with caution (or not).

 Ouch! Be very careful! Totally offensive, completely inappropriate, and downright nasty terms are labeled with this symbol.

We're dealing with real-life French in this book and, therefore, we tell you what the closest English equivalent is so you know when to use each word, phrase, or expression.

Look out for these features throughout the book:

 TOP TIPS on what's incredibly HOT and what's not!

 X-RATED Streetwise SLANG that's really vulgar or SHOCKING.

 Essential COOL FACTS that may seem too cool to be true.

! "I can't believe I said that" and more.. EMBARRASSING STORIES

Finally

You know that language is constantly changing — what's in today may be out tomorrow. So, if you come across anything in this book that's no longer said, or learn a cool expression that hasn't been included, let us know; we'd love to hear from you. Send us an email at language@apaguide.com

This book isn't labeled "Un-Censored" for nothing! This isn't the language you wanna use around your boss, relatives, or your new boy- or girlfriend's parents…got it? The stuff that's in here is pretty hot. If you wanna say it in public, that's up to you. But we are not taking the rap (like responsibility and liability) for any mistakes you make — these include, but are not limited to, verbal abuse, fist fights, smackdowns, and/or arrests that may ensue from your usage of the words and expressions in **Hide This French Book.**

- say hello and good-bye
- ask what's up
- "verlan" explained

1. BASIC
EXPRESSIONS

QUOI DE NEUF?

SALUT!

Hello !
Hello!
In French, say it with an accent on the first syllable.

Salut !
Hi!
It's short and sweet, and works well when you don't know the person already.

Salut, ça va ?
Hi, how are you?
Or - drop the "salut" and just say "ça va" as an alternate greeting.

Hé !
Yo!
A quick way to get someone's attention.

STARTING A CONVERSATION WITH SOMEONE YOU KNOW WOULD GO SOMETHING LIKE THIS..

– **Hé !**   Yo!
– **Salut, ça va ?***   Hi, how are you?
– **Ça va.**   Fine.

*"Ça va" is short for "Comment ça va?" How is it going?
"Ça va" as a response is short for "Ça va bien", It's going well.

PUKER UP!
When greeting each other, the French say "salut" and kiss on both cheeks. In Paris, friends kiss twice — once on each cheek. In other parts of France, friends kiss four times — twice on each cheek starting on the left, then right, left and then right again. This goes for both women and men. Keep in mind that first encounters don't involve any kissing, the rule here is to simply shake hands.

HOW YOU DOIN'?!

– **Quoi de neuf ?*** What's up?
– **Pas grand chose.** Not much.

Literally: What's new?

– **Ça boume ?*** How's it going?
– **Super !** Great!

Literally: Is it blasting? "Boum" is the sound of a French explosion.

– **Ça cartonne ?** Doing well?
– **Carrément !** Totally!

– **Ça va?** How are you?
– **Bien.** Well.

– **Ça gaze ?** Doing well?
– **Comme ci, comme ça.** Sort of. / So so.

– **Ça roule ?*** Doing well?
– **Super !** Great!

Literally: Is it rolling?

quick exits

Ciao ! / Tchao !
Bye!
The Italian "ciao" is so popular the French have taken it over and use it all the time. There's also an alternate, French spelling of the word, "tchao".

Bye-bye !
Bye-bye!
Say it as you would in English!

À plus.
See you later.
This one's short for "à plus tard", see you later. You'll often see it in text messages and e-mails and often written as "A+".

À tout.
See you soon.
This is a quick, cute way to say "à tout à l'heure", literally, within the hour.

FACT

FRENCH HIPSTERS

from the suburbs of Paris started "verlan" — a form of French slang created to confuse the uncool. Verlan works by rearranging the order of letters or syllables of a word. For example, "ça va" becomes "ça av". Instead of explaining the rules, the best examples of verlan have been included throughout this book.

- from chatting up to finishing a relationship
- flatter and flirt with ease
- reject a loser

2. HOOKING UP, BREAKING UP

CASSE-TOI!

JE VOUS OFFRE UN VERRE??

pick-up lines

Voulez-vous vous asseoir ?
Would you like to sit down?
This works wonders in a bar or on the subway.

Je vous offre un verre ?
Can I buy you a drink?
Look confident when using this line.

T'es trop sexy.
You are really sexy.
The perfect informal come-on to use in a bar or club.

CHEESY PICK-UP LINES!

These pick-up lines are cheesy, but they're also great for some laughs. And who knows? They may even work for you!

On se connaît ?
Do we know each other?
You've probably heard this one about a million times…

Pardon, savez-vous où est la poste ?
Excuse-me, do you know where the post office is?
See a hot guy or girl on the street? Try this line to get his or her attention.

Vous êtes mannequin ?
Are you a model?
You'd be surprised how well this one works!

START A CONVERSATION:

– **Je t'offre un verre ?**   Can I buy you a drink?
– **OK, pourquoi pas.**   Sure, why not.

flat-out refusals

Merci, mais j'attends quelqu'un.
Thanks, but I'm expecting someone.
He/She can take a hint.

Va voir ailleurs si j'y suis !
Look elsewhere!
Get your message across without any hassle.

Casse-toi !
Get lost!
Not very nice, but it's crystal clear.

Tu t'es pas regardé !
Take a good look at yourself!
(Literally: You haven't seen yourself!)
It's a no-nonsense approach.

TELL THEM THEY'RE HOT:

Tu es...	You're...
adorable.	very cute.
mignon. ♂	cute.
canon.	hot.
sexy.	sexy.
à tomber. ♂	hot. (Literally: to fall for)
bonne.	good [in bed]. (Literally: good)
chaude. ♀	good [in bed]. (Literally: hot)
un bon coup.	a good lover. (Literally: a good shot)

breaking up

Fallen out of love? Here are the best ways to break it off.

Ça va pas être possible.
It's not going to work out.

C'est fini entre nous.
It's over between us.

Soyons amis.
Let's just be friends.

Je/J'...	I...
romps avec toi.	am breaking up with you.
ai cassé avec lui.	am breaking up with him.
la jette.	am dumping her.
le largue.	am dumping him.

TIP

THE "TEXTO"

Text message: a painless and popular way to dump someone. If you're tired of your boyfriend or girlfriend, you can send him or her a "texto" from your cell phone. You don't even have to talk!

Text Message:	**:---)* Je t'm +. C ni**
French Equivalent:	**Tu es un menteur. Je ne t'aime plus. C'est fini.**
English Translation:	You're a liar. I don't love you anymore. It's over.

*This emoticon—a smiley face with a long nose—means liar.

RATED X

♂ NASTY THINGS TO CALL YOUR EX...

T'es*... You're...

minable.   pathetic.

nul.   a loser.   (Literally: a zero)

une ordure.   a scumbag

un pauvre type.   a bastard.

un vrai connard !   a real bastard!

♀ AND NOT FORGETTING THE GIRLS...

T'es une...   You're a...

HOT! **pouffiasse.**   slut.

EXTRA HOT! **salope.**   bitch.

EXTRA HOT! **vraie connasse !** real bitch!

*"**T'es**" is the quick and easy way to say, "**tu es**", you are.

NO HARD FEELINGS?

– Ça va pas être possible.
It's not going to work out.

– Va te faire foutre ! T'es une vraie ordure.
Fuck you! You're a real scumbag.

or

– Bon. Soyons amis.   Fine. Let's just be friends

- get romantic.. from kissing to sex
- top 10 ways to say we did it
- call someone a cabbage, if you're really in love
- talk about pregnancy and STDs

3. LOVE
and SEX

JE PEUX T'EMBRASSER?

MON AMOUR

in the mood for love?

FIRST COMES THE ATTRACTION...

Ce mec me branche.
I like that guy. (Literally: That guy plugs me in.)

Cette fille, je la kiffe.
I like that girl.

THEN ROMANCE...

J'ai flirté avec lui.
I made out with him.

Je suis sorti avec elle.
I'm going out with her.

Je lui ai roulé un patin.
I french-kissed him. (Literally: I rolled a skate to him.)

FINALLY, SEX!

On s'est mis à poil.
We got naked. (Literally: We wore only our body hair.)

On a pris notre pied.
We had a good time. (Literally: We took our foot.)
Say it with a wink.

BUT, FOR THOSE UNLUCKY IN LOVE...

Elle m'a allumé.
She led me on. (Literally: She lit me.)
Though you can use "allumer" for both sexes, it's usually applied to women. "Une allumeuse" is a tease — definitely used for females only!

J'ai fait la traversée du désert.
I didn't have sex for a long time. (Literally: I went across the desert.)
Is that dry spell over yet?!

sweet talk

Being called a "cabbage" or a "rabbit" is actually quite romantic in French.

Tu es...	You're...
mon amour.	my love.
mon bébé.	my baby.
mon cœur.	my darling. (Literally: my heart)
mon chou.	my dear. (Literally: my cabbage)
mon lapin.	my sweetie. (Literally: my rabbit)
mon trésor.	my treasure.
ma biche.	my doe. ♀

FOREPLAY, ANYONE?!

– **Je peux t'embrasser ?**   Can I kiss you?

– **Bien sûr, mon cœur !**   Of course, my darling!

safe sex

Be careful! You'll probably need these:

J'utilise...	I use...	
des capotes/préservatifs.	condoms.	♂
la pilule.	the pill.	♀
un diaphragme.	a diaphragm.	

PRACTICE YOUR BEDSIDE MANNERS.

- **Tu prends la pilule ?** Are you on the pill?

- **Non. Mets une** No. Put on a condom.
  capote.

STDs 101

Ask the right questions before things get too hot.

Tu as fait un test HIV ?	Have you been tested for HIV?
Tu as...?	Do you have...?
l'hépatite	hepatitis
de l'herpès	herpes
la syphilis	syphilis
le SIDA	AIDS

kinky fun

We've been pretty decent, up until now. So, for those of you who like to party, read on.

N'oublie pas tes...	Don't forget your...
films X / films pornos.	X-rated movies / porno movies.
dessous sexy.	sexy underwear.
menottes.	handcuffs.

RATED X

COUNTLESS WAYS TO SAY WE DID IT

Nous... We...

avons eu des rapports sexuels.   had sexual relations.
It's the medical point of view.

avons passé la nuit ensemble.   spent the night together.
An understatement.

avons couché ensemble. slept together.
Doubt you got any sleep...

avons fait l'amour.   made love.
How romantic!

 avons baisé / avons niqué.   fucked.
Raunchy but right to the point.

AND...

Je/J'... I...
me suis envoyé en l'air.   went to heaven.
Pure bliss.

ai dormi chez lui.   slept at his place.
Who knows what happened...

 ai tiré un coup.   fired a shot. ♂

 l'ai pénétrée.   entered her. ♂

pregnant?

What to say about someone who's expecting...

Elle est enceinte.
She's pregnant.
The standard way to say it.

Marie est en cloque. **HOT!**
Marie got knocked up.
This one's a bit derogatory.

David a engrossé sa copine. **HOT!**
David knocked up his girlfriend.
Not a good thing, in this case...

OOPS!

Brian, an American college student, spent a summer in the south of France with his friend Laurent. To make money, they worked as gardeners at a senior citizens' home. One day, Laurent decided to play a prank on Brian—he asked Brian to get "un seau d'eau misé". A "seau d'eau" is, simply, a bucket of water. But, by adding "misé", Laurent created a very different word: "sodomisé"; literally, sodomite. Needless to say, when Brian asked the senior citizens for "un sodomisé", laughter erupted in the home!

4. GAY and LESBIAN LIFE

SORS DU PLACARD!

IL EST GAY

is he or she gay?

Il est gay / homosexuel.
He's gay.
Elle est lesbienne / homosexuelle.
She's gay.
*use "**Je suis...**" for "I am..."*

C'est...
un pédé.
une pédale.
une tante. (Literally: an aunt)
une grande folle. (Literally: a big crazy woman)

He's gay.

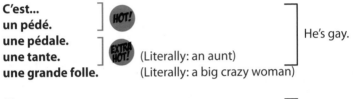

C'est une...
gouine.
brouteuse. (Literally: a nibbler)

She's a lesbian.

Warning! All of these terms can be very offensive and downright rude.

COMING OUT
Fais ton coming out !
Come out of the closet!
Sors du placard !
Get out of the closet!

"GAY PRIDE"
" is the name of a gay-rights demonstration that occurs every June in Paris and other large French cities. Gay men and women parade through the city, some wearing colorful costumes. Straight friends and family also demonstrate their support of gay lifestyles. "Gay Pride" has steadily gained in popularity in France ever since a gay mayor of Paris participated in the event.

- cheer for your team
- talk about soccer
- in the gym
- feeling good, or not
- gambling and the hottest games

5. SPORT
and GAMES

EXTRA, CE BUT!

ALLEZ!

cheers

cheers from "les supporteurs" (the fans)

Allez !
Go!

On y va !
Let's go!

Tous ensemble !
All together!

Bouffez-les ! / Explosez-les !
Get them! (Literally: Eat them! / Explode them!)

On est les champions !
We are the champions!

compliments

Use these expressions to celebrate your team's spectacular moves and shots during the game.

Bravo, le gardien !
Cheers to the goalkeeper!

Divin, ce drible !
Divine dribble!

Magnifique passe !
Beautiful pass!

Extra, ce but !
Great goal!

Quel match génial !
What a great match!

insults

Don't forget that harassing the referee, "l'arbitre", and humiliating the opponent, "l'adversaire", is part of your job as a spectator

Vendu, l'arbitre !
The referee took a bribe! (Literally: Paid for!)

Retourne au vestiaire ! / Aux chiottes !
Kick him out! (Literally: Go to the locker room! / In the bathroom!)

C'est un hold-up !
They missed their chance! (Literally: It's a hold-up!)

Immanquable !
How could you miss that?! (Literally: Can't be missed!)

Téléphoné !
So predictable! (Literally: Telephoned!)

Va te coucher / rhabiller !
You suck! (Literally: Go to bed / get dressed!)

Quel nul !
He sucks! (Literally: What a zero!)

Il n'a pas fait le voyage pour rien !
What a mistake! (Literally: He didn't travel for nothing!)

Quel enculé ! / Quel merde, ce joueur !
Fuck this player!

EXTRA HOT!

i love soccer

Soccer is by far the most popular sport in France, both to watch and to play. "Les Bleus" are the national team, and the French absolutely adore them.

Mets...	Put on...
un maillot.	a jersey.
un short.	shorts.
des protèges tibia.	shin guards.
des crampons.	soccer cleats [boots].
Fais une passe !	Pass the ball!
Attention au numéro quatre !	Watch player number four!
Dégueulasse !	Foul!
Penalty !	Penalty kick!
But !	Goal!

BUT, THERE'S MORE TO LIFE THAN SOCCER...

Je fais...	I...
du vélo.	cycle.
du jogging.	jog.
du roller.	rollerblade.
du skate.	skateboard.
du surf.	surf.
de la natation.	swim.
Tu veux jouer au...?	Do you want to play...?
basket	basketball
tennis	tennis
volley	volleyball

extreme sports

Je veux faire...	I want to go...
du saut en parachute.	skydiving.
du kayak.	kayaking.
de l'alpinisme.	mountain-climbing.
du rafting.	rafting.
du saut à l'élastique.	bungee jumping.

TIP

THE SCOOP

The "Kop" are fanatical followers of French sports teams — they paint their faces with the team colors, wave banners during games, and stand up to cheer their favorite moves or boo the opposition and the referee's bad calls.

ARE YOU UP FOR A CHALLENGE?

– **Tu veux faire du saut en parachute ?**	Want to go skydiving?
– **Pas question !**	No way!
or	
– **J'adorerais ça !**	I'd love to!

working out in the gym

Je peux faire des haltères ?	Can I use the weights?
Je peux utiliser...?	Can I use...?
le vélo de salle	the fitness bike
le rameur	the rowing machine
le tapis de course	the treadmill
Tu veux essayer...?	Do you want to try...?
la boxe française	French boxing*
le judo	judo
le karaté	karate
le vélo sur piste	spinning
le tai chi chuan	tai chi
'aqua gym	water aerobics
le yoga	yoga
Je dois...	I must...
m'échauffer.	warm-up.
m'étirer.	stretch.
ralentir.	slow down.

*In French boxing, you use your feet to kick in addition to punching with your hands.

ready to sweat

The French are always fashion conscious — even at the gym.
Here's the lowdown on the right exercise attire.

Tu as...?	Do you have...?
une brassière	a sports bra
un suspensoir	a jock strap (Literally: a suspender)
un débardeur	a tank top
un tee-shirt	a T-shirt
un sweat-shirt	a sweatshirt
un survêtement / un jogging	sweats
des tennis / des baskets	sneakers

AND, DON'T BE CAUGHT DEAD IN THE WRONG WORKOUT CLOTHES:

Regarde, il porte...!	Look, he's wearing...!
un bandeau	a headband
des jambières	leg warmers
des chaussettes noires et des tennis	black socks with sneakers

pumped up or worn out?

FEELING GOOD...

J'ai la pêche.
I feel great. (Literally: I have the peach.)

Je suis en forme.
I feel great/ I'm fit.

FEELING AWFUL...

J'ai un coup de pompe.
I'm feeling tired. (Literally: I've been hit by a pump.)

Je suis naze.
I'm tired.

Je suis crevé / mort.
I'm dead tired.

J'en peux plus.
I can't take it anymore.

J'en ai plein le dos / le cul.
I'm sick of it. (Literally: I have my back / ass full.)

Tip: all of the above terms can be used in day-to-day life
to express energy levels, whether you're at work, school or
heading out for a night on the town.

video games

If you're a video game aficionado, you'll feel at ease with French games — much of the terms used in English are also applied in French. They even have English terms to name game tools, equipment, and commands.

Où est...?	Where's the...?
l'ordinateur	computer
le joystick	joystick
la Xbox®	Xbox®
On joue...?	Wanna play...?
aux jeux vidéo	video games
à la gameboy®	Game Boy®
à la gamecube™	GameCube™
à la playstation®	PlayStation®
Tu aimes les jeux...?	Do you like...games?
d'action	action
d'aventure	adventure
de sport	sports

SOCCER

Soccer is so popular that it's played both outside and inside. "FIFA Soccer" is a hugely popular video game — you're the coach, and must lead your team through matches and championships. You'll need to acquire the right players, figure out the best gaming strategy, and direct your team during the matches. "FIFA Soccer" is updated every year, includes cool commentaries, and comes with a rockin' soundtrack.

play the game

Vise !	Aim!
Tire !	Shoot!
Tue-le !	Get him!
Fonce !	Quick!
Saute !	Jump!
Marque !	Score!
Il me reste une vie ?	Do I have another man?
Rallume !	Restart!
Game over.	Game over.

gambling

Tu veux...?	Do you want to...?
parier	bet
miser	bid
risquer le paquet	put all your money down
jouer à pile ou face	flip a coin
Tu as...?	Did you...?
perdu au jeu	gamble it away
tout perdu	lose it all
remporté la mise	win the hand

card games

Tu veux jouer...?	Do you want to play...?
aux cartes	cards
au rami	gin
au poker	poker
On se fait...?	Wanna play...?
une belote	belote*
un tarot	tarot

J'ai la main.
I have the deal. (Literally: I have the hand).

Tu veux couper ?
Do you want to cut [the deck]?

Je me couche.
I fold. (Literally: I'm going to sleep.)

say it with cards...

The French have such a fondness for cards that they've incorporated them into daily usage.

Abats tes cartes !
Reveal your intentions! (Literally: Show your cards!)

Joue cartes sur table.
Tell the truth. (Literally: Put your cards on the table.)

Ne brouille pas les cartes !
Don't complicate things! (Literally: Don't mix the cards!)

C'est ta dernière carte.
This is your last chance. (Literally: You played your last card.)

* "La belote" has been the unofficial national game of France for almost a century and is so popular it's even featured in some French gangster films. It's easy to play; the object of the game is simply to hold on to as many cards as possible.

FACT

"LE TAROT"

In France, unless you're in a fortune-teller's salon, "le tarot" refers to an old and widely played card game. French tarot has a unique deck: in addition to the usual deck of 52 cards, it has four "cavaliers", riders, between the queens and jacks. It also has 21 trumps, numbered from one ("le petit", the little) to 21 ("le 21"). The point of the game is to gain as many points as possible by holding onto the royalty, in other words, the jacks, queens, and kings.

6.SHOPPING

TIP

CHIC BOUTIQUES

In Paris, it's not only the clothes that are cool—the stores are ultra hip too. You'll find chic boutiques, many with their own design theme (lounge, urban, or even zen) and some with fully-stocked cafés, funky art exhibitions, and DJs spinning the latest tunes. These concept stores carry the newest, soon-to-be coolest, products. Many of the trendsetting items sold in these stores can also be found online.

shop talk

Je cherche...	I'm looking for...
une boutique.	a boutique.
un grand magasin.	a department store.
un magasin de marques dégriffés.	an outlet store.
une boutique d'articles d'occasion.	a second-hand store.
une boutique de fringues vintage.	a vintage shop.
un marché aux puces.	a flea market.
un marché.	a market.

On va faire des courses ?
Are we going shopping?

Tu veux faire du lèche-vitrine ?
Do you want to go window-shopping?

FACT

BEFORE YOU GET TOO CARRIED AWAY..

The French rarely use credit cards and instead prefer to pay in cash or by "carte bleue"(debit card). Not to worry though — most credit cards are widely accepted too but you'll need a PIN and you may be asked to show some ID.

NEED SOME HELP? ASK "LA VENDEUSE", THE SALES CLERK.

Où se trouve...?	Where's...?
le rayon femme	the women's department
le rayon lingerie	the lingerie department
le rayon homme	the men's department
le rayon enfant	the children's department
la cabine d'essayage	the fitting room
le rayon chaussures	the shoe department
le rayon parfumerie	the perfume / cosmetics department
le rayon bijouterie	the jewelry department
la caisse	the register
le service clientèle	customer service
Où se trouvent...?	Where are...?
les accessoires	the accessories
les toilettes	the restrooms
Où se trouve la cabine d'essayage ?	Where's the fitting room?
Là-bas.	Over there.
Merci !	Thanks!

CONFRONTED BY AN ANNOYING SALES CLERK?
- **Bonjour, je peux vous aider ?** Hi, can I help you?
- **Je regarde, merci.** I'm just browsing, thanks.
- **D'accord.** OK.

"les fringues" (clothing)

Où trouver...?	Where can I find...?
un pantalon pattes d'éléphant	boot-cut pants
un pantalon taille basse	low-rise pants
un polo	a polo shirt
un pantalon moulant	stretchy pants
un jean	jeans
une mini-jupe	a miniskirt
une veste en cuir	a leather jacket
Je cherche...	I'm looking for...
un sac à dos.	a backpack.
des livres / magazines.	books / magazines.
des CD / DVD.	CDs / DVDs.
des cartes de vœux.	greeting cards.
...sont branché(e)s.	...are in.
Les pantacourts	capri pants
Les rayures	stripes
Les tee-shirts très décolletés	ultra low-cut T-shirts
Les wonderbras	Wonderbras®
Les balconnets*	underwire bras

*It's the quick way to say, "soutiens-gorge à balconnets", underwire bras.

how much?

C'est en solde ?	Is this on sale?
C'est combien ?	How much is it?
Ça raque.	It's pricey. (Literally: It pays.)
C'est reuch.	It's expensive.

"Reuch" is "verlan" or slang for "cher".

C'est trop cher !	It's too expensive!
Vous me faites une remise ?	Can you give me a discount?
Vous me faites un prix ?	Will you lower the price?
Quel bon plan !	What a good deal!
Quelle escroquerie !	What a rip-off!
Je regarde.	I'm just browsing.
Je vais réfléchir.	I'll think about it.
Je reviendrai.	I'll come back.

FACT

RETURNS

Shopping in France may be fun, but who said it was easy? If you're not happy with your purchase, few stores will give you your money back — at best, you'll get a store credit. And you better decide quickly — you usually only have a few days to make an exchange.

TIP

PRICE TAG

In France, the price you see on the tag is the price you pay: taxes are already included. "Les soldes", sales, happen only twice a year, after New Year's and in July. It is illegal to have "des soldes" in between these periods. However, you might find "des promotions", discounts on specific items in any store, at various times of the year.

The only places to use your bargaining power are at "les marchés aux puces", flea markets, and "les marchés", markets, which are usually outdoors and move from neighborhood to neighborhood.

money, money, money

Passe-moi...

du blé. (Literally: wheat)

du fric.

du pèse.

du pognon.

Gimme some money.

flat broke

Je suis fauché.
I'm broke. (Literally: I'm mowed.)

C'est la dèche.
I have no money.

Je peux te taper une pièce ?
Can I borrow some money? (Literally: Can I hit you for some money?)

- fashion talk
- what's in your wardrobe
- hiar and make-up
- body art and alterations

7. FASHION

in vogue

Tu es tellement...!	You're so...!
in	in (say it as you would in English)
branché	trendy (Literally: plugged in)
tendance	trendy
BCBG*	preppy

* BCBG stands for "Bon Chic Bon Genre", the right kind of chic, the right kind of genre. This one can be used a little pejoratively though so take caution with the tone used when saying it!)

fashion disaster

Ce style est complètement...	This style is completely...
niais.	cheesy.
clinquant.	gaudy.
ringard / depassé.	out.
tape à l'œil.	tacky. (Literally: hitting your eye)

TIP

WHAT DO GIRLS WEAR GOING CLUBBING?

The trick is to look sexy, yet not too provocative and to wear something that's comfortable for dancing. You'll find that in France, girls prefer pants to skirts, especially pants with a little stretch in them.

A tank top would look nice, but most girls avoid backless tops in order to keep the guys at arm's length. And, of course, many wear high heels—they're the ultimate touch for a sexy figure. Guys, on the other hand, wear the standard club outfit: jeans, cool T-shirt, leather or suede jacket, and casual shoes or dressy sneakers.

wardrobe essentials

une casquette de baseball
baseball cap

un tee-shirt moulant
tight T-shirt

une veste en jean
denim jacket

un jean
jeans

un slip
briefs

un pull
sweater

une besace / un sac à bandoulière
messenger bag

des pompes / des chouzes
shoes

un caleçon
boxers

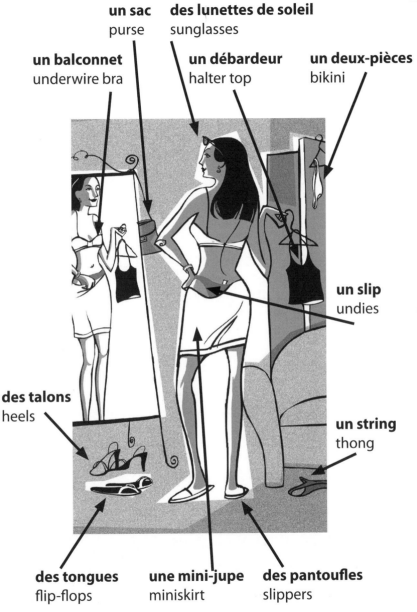

un sac
purse

des lunettes de soleil
sunglasses

un balconnet
underwire bra

un débardeur
halter top

un deux-pièces
bikini

un slip
undies

des talons
heels

un string
thong

des tongues
flip-flops

une mini-jupe
miniskirt

des pantoufles
slippers

le maquillage (make up)

J'ai besoin de/d'...	I need some...
blush.	blush.
fond de teint.	foundation.
eye liner.	eyeliner.
ombre à paupières.	eye shadow.
gloss / rouge à lèvres.	lipgloss / lipstick.
mascara.	mascara.
poudre.	powder

in the powder room

Don't forget about those toiletry essentials! Just keep your language fresh and clean.

J'ai besoin de...	I need...
mon déodorant.	my deodorant.
ma crème.	my lotion.
mes serviettes hygiéniques.	my pads.
mes tampons.	my tampons.
ma trousse.	my make-up bag.

SOLVE BATHROOM ISSUES WITH EASE.

–Tu me passes du papier toilette ?	Can you give me some toilet paper?
–Le voilà.	Here you are.

YOU CAN FIND GREAT PRODUCTS..

..and great deals — at supermarkets such as "Monoprix" and Carrefour. In addition to medicine and perfume, you can purchase make-up and other essentials at "une pharmacie", a pharmacy. Or check out "une parfumerie", a shop that sells make-up and perfume brands. "Sephora" is a really popular "parfumerie" that has locations worldwide and all over France.

make yourself beautiful

Je voudrais...	I'd like...
un nettoyage de peau.	a facial.
une manucure.	a manicure.
une pédicure / beauté des pieds.	a pedicure.
un massage.	a massage.
une épilation du maillot.	a bikini wax.
une épilation des sourcils.	an eyebrow wax.
une épilation des jambes entières.	a full-leg wax.

Je voudrais me faire les ongles des mains et des pieds.
I want a manicure and pedicure.

MOST FRENCH WOMEN DON'T SHAVE, THEY WAX.

Some wax at home; others visit the beauty salon. You'll have to plan your trip "chez l'esthéticienne" ahead of time and make an appointment; walk-ins usually aren't accepted. The esthetician will do everything from your toes to your arms and eyebrows, not to mention "le maillot", bikini, and "les aisselles", underarms. And, you don't need to tip, unless you've received superior service.

crowning glory

J'ai besoin de/d'...	I need...
une frange.	bangs.
un brushing.	a blow out.
une coupe de cheveux.	a hair cut.
mèches.	highlights.
Tu as...?	Do you have...?
une barrette	a barette
un serre-tête	a headband
des pinces à cheveux	hair clips
un élastique	a hairband
une épingle à cheveux	a hairpin
Elle a les cheveux...	Her hair is...
bouclés.	curly.
raides.	straight.
teints.	dyed.
décolorés.	lightened.
blonds / bruns / roux / noirs.	blond / brown / red / black.
Il a...	He has...
une barbe.	a beard.
une coupe en brosse.	a buzz cut.
un bouc.	a goatee.
une barbe de trois jours.	scruff. (Literally: a beard of three days)
la boule à zéro.	a completely shaved head. (Literally: a zero ball)

body work

Tu as fait de la chirurgie esthétique ?
Have you had plastic surgery?

Je me suis fait refaire...	I had...
les seins.	a boob job.
le nez.	a nose job.
le ventre.	a tummy tuck.

Je me suis fait gonfler les lèvres.
I had my lips enhanced.

Il s'est fait tatouer.
He got a tattoo.

Il a un piercing au...	He has a/an...piercing.
nombril.	belly button
sourcil.	eyebrow
téton.	nipple
nez.	nose

If you decide to get a piercing or tattoo in France, be prepared.
Here's how to say —or scream — that it hurts.

Oh lala...	Oh boy...
Aïe !	Ouch!
Ouille !	Ow!
Beuh !	Ugh!
Berk !	Yikes!

8. BODY

body beautiful

Tu as...	You have...
de jolies jambes.	nice legs.
les fesses fermes.	a tight butt.
de beaux seins.	nice boobs.
un corps parfait.	a perfect body.
Je/J'...	I...
ai du bide.	have a beer gut.
ai des bourrelets.	have stomach rolls.
suis plate.	am flat-chested.
porte des lunettes.	wear glasses.
porte des verres de contact.	wear contacts.

who's your type?

J'aime les hommes...	I like...men.
musclés.	muscular
petit / grands.	short / tall
chauves / poilus.	bald / hairy
aux cheveux longs.	long-haired
barbus.	bearded
avec une barbe de trois jours.	scruffy
J'aime les filles...	I like...girls.
menues.	petite
avec des formes.	curvy
grandes.	tall
aux cheveux courts.	short-haired
avec une grosse poitrine.	big-breasted

lookin' hot—or not

ALL ABOUT HER... ♀

C'est un boudin.
She is an ugly woman. (Literally: She is blood sausage.)
It may sound corny, but this is a real insult in French!

Elle est plate comme une limande.
She's flat-chested. (Literally: She's as flat as a flounder.)
Ouch!

Elle a de la culotte de cheval.
She has saddlebags.
(that would be those rolls of fat around the thigh area)

C'est une grande perche.
She is tall and skinny. (Literally: She is a string bean.)
This comment isn't meant to be positive.

Elle est bien roulée.
She has a nice body. (Literally: She's well-curved.)

Il y a du monde au balcon.
She has big boobs. (Literally: The balcony is crowded.)
It's said when a woman's cleavage is a little too visible.

ALL ABOUT HIM... ♂

Quel gros lard!
What a fat slob! (Literally: What a fat piece of bacon!)

Il est maigre comme un clou.
He is skin and bones. (Literally: He is skinny as a nail.)
Some may find this characteristic appealing...

Quel beau gosse.
What a handsome guy. (Literally: What a handsome kid.)

Il est bien foutu.
He has a great body. (Literally: He's well-made.)

Il est baraqué.
He is well-built. (Literally: He is built like a house.)

Il est carrément sexy.
He is so sexy.

Il a de la gueule.
He is striking.

ALL ABOUT HIM OR HER...

C'est un beau morceau.
He/She is a handsome morsel.
Absolutely delicious, right?!

Quel canon !
What a knock-out!
It's usually said with the mouth wide open.

OOPS!

A young American man was living in Paris for a year. He loved doing his shopping in the little stores around his neighborhood — especially the butcher's, since it was run by women. One day he decided to try one of their specialties, blood sausage. But instead of saying, "Vous avez du boudin ?", Do you have blood sausage? he said, "vous êtes un boudin", you are an ugly woman; literally, you are a blood sausage — quite an insult in French. He had to find a different butcher from then on!

wardrobe essentials

HOT! *WARNING! THE LANGUAGE ON THIS PAGE CAN BE PRETTY HOT!*

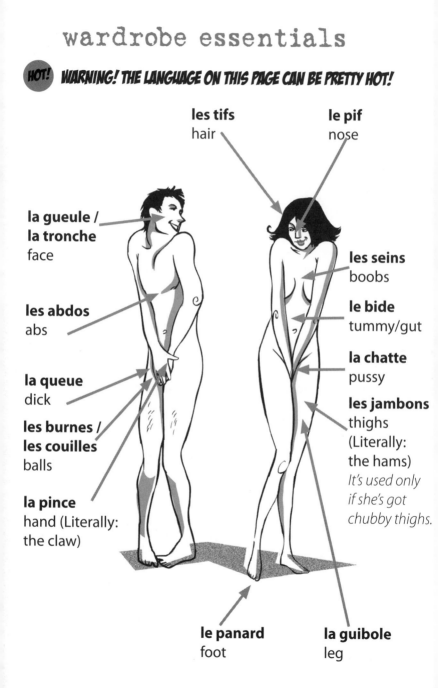

les tifs
hair

le pif
nose

**la gueule /
la tronche**
face

les seins
boobs

les abdos
abs

le bide
tummy/gut

la chatte
pussy

la queue
dick

les jambons
thighs
(Literally:
the hams)
*It's used only
if she's got
chubby thighs.*

**les burnes /
les couilles**
balls

la pince
hand (Literally:
the claw)

le panard
foot

la guibole
leg

body functions

and here's the lowdown on the less glamourous bits...

J'ai besoin de...	I have to...
roter.	burp.
chier.	crap.
péter.	fart.
pisser.	piss.
dégueuler.	puke.
gerber.	throw-up.
	Say it in verlan: "béger".

HOT!

Tu pues la transpiration !
You've got BO! (Literally: You reek of perspiration!)

Tu schlingues!
You stink!

J'ai...	I have...
de l'acné.	acne.
des points noirs.	blackheads.
un bouton.	a pimple.
une mauvaise haleine.	bad breath.
une verrue.	a wart.
une éruption de boutons.	a rash.
des crampes.	cramps.
des crampes au ventre.	menstrual cramps.
des pertes.	discharge.
la diarrhée.	diarrhea.
les pieds qui puent.	smelly feet.

- phone friends and send text messages
- get connected online: e-mail, Facebook, Twitter, and chat rooms
- fall in love with web personals

9. TECHNOLOGY

C'EST MOI!

ON S'APPELLE!

call me

Je peux...?	Can I...?
prendre ton numéro	get your number
t'appeler	call you
passer un coup de fil	make a phone call

phone talk

Allô ?
Hello?
Say this when you answer the phone.

Oui.
Yes.
If you don't want to say "Allô?" try this.

Salut !
Hey!
If you know who's on the other end, feel free to be very informal.

C'est Michel.
It's Michel.
The standard way to identify yourself on the phone.

C'est moi !
It's me!
Everybody knows you, right?

Est-ce que je pourrais parler à Francine ?
Could I speak with Francine?
Formal, but to the point.

Je peux laisser un message ?
Can I leave a message?
Be polite, for once!

J'y vais.
Gotta go.
In a hurry? End your conversation with this one.

À plus.
Later.
The perfect ending to any conversation.

Je t'embrasse.
Love you. (Literally: I kiss you.)
Use this one with friends and family.

On s'appelle.
Let's talk later.
Warning: this can mean "I won't call you".

A FRIENDLY PHONE CONVERSATION MIGHT START SOMETHING LIKE THIS...
- **Allô ?**   Hello?
- **Salut. C'est Alain.**   Hi. It's Alain.
- **Salut, Alain! Quoi de neuf ?**   Hey Alain! What's up? .

answering machines

Vous êtes bien chez Georges. Laissez un message après le bip.
This is George. Leave a message after the beep.

Salut, c'est Sylvie! Appelle-moi !
Hi, it's Sylvie! Call me!

texting

In France, almost everybody has "un portable", a cell phone. Calls are pricey, so many people send and receive "textos" instead.

je t'M	[Je t'aime.]	*I love you.*
Cpa5p	[C'est pas sympa.]	*That's not nice.*

rstp	[Réponds s'il te plaît.]	*Answer please.*
keske C	[Qu'est-ce que c'est?]	*What is it?*
@2m1	[À demain.]	*See you tomorrow.*

A CONVERSATION BY TEXT MIGHT GO SOMETHING LIKE THIS..

slt cv ?	Salut, ça va ?	*Hi, how are you?*
m jvb	Moi, je vais bien.	*I'm fine.*
koi29 ?	Quoi de neuf ?	*What's up?*
RAS	Rien à signaler.	*Nothing.*
tu vi1 2m'1	Tu viens demain ?	*Are you coming tomorrow?*
je C pas j'tapL + tard	Je sais pas. Je t'appelle plus tard.	*I don't know. I'll call you later.*

online

Où y-a-t-il un cyber café ?
Where's an internet cafe?

Est-ce qu'il a la connexion Wi-Fi ?
Does it have wireless internet?

Quel est le mot de passe du WiFi ?
What is the WiFi password?

Est-ce que le WiFi est gratuit ?
Is the WiFi free?

Avez-vous Bluetooth ?
Do you have bluetooth?

Je vais...	I'm going to...
me connecter (à Internet).	go on-line.
surfer (sur le web).	surf (the web).

envoyer un e-mail*.	send an e-mail.
télécharger la pièce jointe.	download the attachment.
Puis-je brancher / charger mon ordinateur portable / iPhone / iPad ?	Can I plug in/charge my laptop/iPhone/iPad/BlackBerry?
Puis-je accéder à Skype ?	Can I access Skype?
Combien coûte la demi-heure/ l'heure ?	How much per half hour/ hour?
Tu peux…?	Can you…?
te connecter / déconnecter	sign on / sign off
Comment est-ce que…?	How do I…?
j'ouvre/je termine la session	log on/off
je frappe ce symbole	type this symbol
Quel est votre mail?	What's your e-mail?
Mon mail est…	My e-mail is…
Tu peux m'envoyer un e-mail?	Can you send me an e-mail?
Quel est…préféré(e)?	**What's your favorite…?**
ton navigateur	**browser**
ton chatroom	**chatroom**
ta page d'accueil	**homepage**
ton forum	**newsgroup**
ta page web	**webpage**
ton site	**website**
IM / dialoguer en direct	**IM someone**

* "Courriel" and "mèl" are terms also used for e-mail.

key words

ordinateur / ordi.	computer.
machine.	machine.
clavier.	keyboard.
portable.	laptop.
souris.	mouse.
écran.	screen.
joindre une pièce	attach a document
dérouler le texte	scroll up / down
Allume-le.	Turn it on.
Clique ici !	Click here!
Efface !	Delete!
Appuie sur entrée / échapper.	Press return / escape.
N'oublie pas de sauvegarder.	Don't forget to save.
Tu dois sortir / redémarrer.	You need to logout / reboot.
Mon ordi a planté. **Éteins-le.**	My computer crashed. Turn it off.

social media

Es-tu sur Facebook/Twitter ?	Are you on Facebook/ Twitter?
Quel est ton nom d'utilisateur?	What's your user name?
Je t'ajouterai comme ami.	I'll add you as a friend.
Je te suivrai sur Twitter.	I'll follow you on Twitter.
Suis-tu...?	Are you following...?
Je mettrai les photos sur Facebook/Twitter.	I'll put the pictures on Facebook/Twitter.

Je te marquerai sur les photos.
I'll tag you in the pictures.
Je vous marquerai sur les photos. (plural form)

acronyms

If you want to join a French chat, text or instant message/
Facebook a French friend, you'd better know some shorthand…

ASV [age, sexe, ville]
A/S/L [age, sex, location]
Start your chat by asking about 'em.

BAN [chasser d'une chat room]
BAN [to ban from a chat room]

MDR [mort de rire]
LOL [laugh out loud] (Literally: dead from laughing)

PSEUDO [pseudonyme]
NICK [nickname]
*Most popular French NICKs include: "Captain [name]," "Doctor
[name]," "Maverick," "Réplicants".*

kékina [Qu'est-ce qu'il y a ?]
RUOK [Are you OK?] (Literally: What's the matter?)

dak [D'accord.]
OK

c ça [C'est ça !]
Really! (Literally: That's it!)

l'S tomB [Laisse tomber.]
NP [No problem.] (Literally: Drop it.)

@+ [À plus.]
CUL8R [See you later.]

@2m1 [À demain.]
CUT [See you tomorrow.]

A12C4 [À un de ces quatre.]
CU [See you.] (Literally: See you one of these [four] days.)

instant messaging

slt koi29?
(Salut. Quoi de neuf ?)
Hi, what's up?

1mn. Je V o 6n .
(Juste une minute. Je vais au ciné.)
I only have a minute. I'm going to the movies.

BAP.
(Bon après-midi.)
Have a good time.

j tapLDkej pe.
(Je t'appelle dès que je peux.)
I'll call you as soon as I can.

e-mail

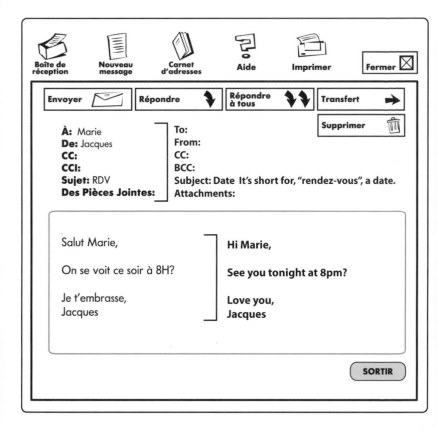

Boîte de réception   **Nouveau message**   **Carnet d'adresses**   **Aide**   **Imprimer**   Fermer

Envoyer   **Répondre**   **Répondre à tous**   **Transfert**

Supprimer

À: Marie
De: Jacques
CC:
CCI:
Sujet: RDV
Des Pièces Jointes:

To:
From:
CC:
BCC:
Subject: Date It's short for, "rendez-vous", a date.
Attachments:

Salut Marie,

On se voit ce soir à 8H?

Je t'embrasse,
Jacques

Hi Marie,

See you tonight at 8pm?

Love you,
Jacques

SORTIR

online dating

LOOKING FOR THAT SPECIAL GUY..

Salut les garçons, si vous êtes canons, vous avez entre 20-25 et vivez à Paris, appelez-moi aussi vite que possible pour discuter et prendre mon cœur.

Hi guys; if you're hot, between 20 and 25, and living in Paris, call me to talk and take my heart.

and here it is in short..

```
slt les mek, si vous  tes Knon 20-25 dans le 75 apLER
moi asap pr10kuT + prendre mon keur.
```

Bonjour. Tu as entre 18 et 25 ans, tu es belle et sympa, je t'aime déjà. Réponds s'il te plaît.

Hello. You are between 18 and 25, beautiful and nice; I love you already. Answer please.

and here it is in short..

```
Bjr. t a 18-25, BL   5pa, je t m Dja. rstp.
```

LOOKING FOR THAT SPECIAL GIRL..

Mec 25 ans, cherche femme pour dialoguer en direct et plus si possible. Laissez-moi un message.

25-year-old guy looking for woman to talk to and more if possible. Leave me a message.

and in short…

```
Mek 25 cherche fam pr chat   + si posibl. LC moi 1
msg.
```

- talk about your friends
- gossip and secrets
- talk about your family
- insult someone's mother

10. FRIENDS
AND FAMILY

TU RIGOLES!

JE PEUX PAS LE CROIRE!

best of friends

Lui c'est mon...	He is my...
ami.	friend.
pote / poteau.	buddy.
C'est ma meilleure amie.	Elle est adorable!
She's my best friend.	She's such a sweetheart!
Tu es vraiment sympa.	C'est un mec super.
You're really nice.	He's a cool guy.

ex-friends

Je peux pas le blairer.
I can't stand him.

Je peux pas la piffrer.
I can't stand her.
"Piffrer" is a slang term meaning to smell.

Il...	He...
me tape sur les nerfs.	gets on my nerves.
me fait suer.	pisses me off. (Literally: makes me sweat)
m'emmerde.	annoys the shit out of me.

DON'T BE AFRAID TO BE HONEST.
– **Tu connais Marc ?** Do you know Marc?
– **Je peux pas le blairer !** I can't stand him!

what a dumb ass

Il est con comme un manche à balai.
He's as dumb as a doornail.
(Literally: He's as stupid as a [broom] stick.)

Quel...	What a/an...
bouffon.	fool.
débile / gogol.	idiot.
tache.	idiot. (Literally: stain)
naze.	loser.
con / blaireau.	jerk.

Je l'ai en horreur !
I hate him!

Je la déteste !
I detest her!

Il me donne envie de vomir !
He makes me want to puke!

gossip

Je peux pas le croire !	I can't believe it!
Sans blague.	No kidding. (Literally: Without a joke.)
Sans dec !	No kidding!
Tu déconnes ?!	Are you kidding me?!
Tu rigoles !	You're joking! (Literally: You're laughing!)
Tu plaisantes !	You're joking!
Oh lala !	Oh boy!
Non !	No!

La vache !	No shit! (Literally: The cow!)
con / blaireau.	jerk.
Je l'ai en horreur !	I hate him!
Je la déteste !	I detest her!
Il me donne de vomir !	He makes me want to puke!

BE HONEST.
– **Quel con, ce mec !** What a jerk he is!
– **Sans dec* !** No kidding!

*"Dec" is short for "déconner", to fool around.

say it as it is

J'en ai...	I've had...
assez.	enough.
ma claque.	enough. (Literally: my slap)
ras le bol.	it. (Literally: my bowl full)
Tu es complètement...	You are totally...
ouf.	crazy. It's verlan for "fou", crazy.
dérangé.	deranged.
tarré.	disturbed.
destroy.	nuts.
barjo.	wacky.
Tu es si...	You're so...
énervant.	annoying.

arrogant.	arrogant.
orgueilleux.	conceited.
grossier.	rude.

Quel péteux !
What a snot!

Ce mec est chelou.
That guy is shady.
"Chelou" is verlan for "louche", shady.

Cette fille est une salope.
That girl is a bitch.

SOME FRIENDLY BANTER...
– **Con !** Jerk!
– **Écrase !** Shut up!

RATED X

YOU'VE JUST BEEN INSULTED?
HERE ARE THE BEST WAYS TO REACT.

Tu me gonfles !
You're getting on my nerves!
(Literally: You make me swell!)

T'as pas d'amis.
You have no friends.

T'es relou.
Gimme a break. (Literally: You're heavy.)
"Relou" is verlan for "lourd", heavy.

Écrase !
Shut up! (Literally: Crush it!)

C'est con pour toi !
It sucks to be you! (Literally: It's too bad for you!)

Nimportenawaque !
Whatever!
Don't let this word scare you! It's another way to say
"n'importe quoi", what nonsense.

Tu es un loser.
You're a real loser.

Va te faire foutre !
Fuck you!

be a good friend

Calmos.
Calm down.
Have your pal take some deep breaths, too.

Cool !
Cool down!
Has your friend totally lost it? Try this.

Cool ma poule.
Cool down, girl. (Literally: Cool down, my hen.)

Relax !
Relax!
Say it when a friend's all worked up about something.

T'inquiète.
Don't worry.

secrets

Ne dis rien.
Don't tell.

Tu promets de ne rien dire ?
Promise not to tell?

Tu peux garder un secret ?
Can you keep a secret?

Garde-le pour toi.
Keep it to yourself.

Tu peux me faire confiance.
You can trust me.

family ties

Voici...	This is my...
mon demi-frère.	half-brother.
ma demi-sœur.	half-sister.
le fils de mon beau-père. (Literally: the son of my stepfather)	
le fils de ma belle-mère. (Literally: the son of my stepmother)	step-brother.
la fille de mon beau-père. (Literally: the daughter of my stepfather)	step-sister.
la fille de ma belle-mère. (Literally: the daughter of my stepmother)	
mon beau-père.	stepfather.
ma belle-mère.	stepmother.

family slang

Je ne peux pas sentir...	I can't stand my...
ma mifa.	family.
mes remps.	parents.
mon reup.	father.
ma reum.	mother.
mon reuf.	brother.
ma reuss.	sister.

POKE SOME FUN AT YOUR FAMILY!

– **Ta belle-doch a des gamins ?**
  Your stepmother has kids?
– **Ouais, trois merdeux !** Yeah, three brats!

J'adore...	I love my...
mes vieux.	folks. (Literally: my old)
ma belle-doch.	stepmother.
mon frangin.	brother.
ma frangine.	sister.

Ce gamin est énervant.
This kid is annoying.

Quels merdeux !
What brats!

Tu es une vraie chipie.
You're a real brat.

TIP

DORMITORIES..

In France, few colleges have dormitories; the custom is to go to college close to home. As a result, if you live in a big city, you stay at home during your studies.

FOR WHEN YOU'VE REALLY HAD ENOUGH

Watch out! Be careful with these expressions; you could make enemies for life, they're hardcore. Insulting someone's mother is a grave offense. If you're really pissed at someone, these ones always hit below the belt.

Ta mère !
Your mother!

Fils de pute !
Son of a bitch!

Ta mère, la pute !
Your mother, the whore!

Rentre chez ta mère !
Go home to your mother!

Nique ta mère !
Fuck your mother!

Va voir ta mère !
Go and fuck your mother!

11. FOOD

hungry?

J'ai...!	I am...!
faim	hungry
la dalle	starving
les crocs	famished (Literally: the fangs)
soif	thirsty
J'ai envie de...	I want to...
bouffer.	eat.
bâfrer.	eat a lot.
damer.	pig out. (Literally: ram)
m'empiffrer.	stuff myself.
Il mange comme quatre.	He eats like a pig. (Literally: He eats like four.)
Je cale.	I'm full.
J'ai trop bouffé.	I ate too much.
Je meurs de faim / de soif !	I'm dying of hunger / thirst!

FAST FOOD.

Traditional French cuisine has been known for its high fat content. Today, some French are indulging in other types of fatty meals—fast food! Once, the typical afternoon snack was a piece of freshly baked bread with a small bar of chocolate. Now, candy bars and chips are big, and soda consumption has skyrocketed. Fast food joints are totally in.

dining out

On va...	Let's go to...
au self.	a buffet. *It's short for: "self-service".*
au café.	a cafe.
à la cafet.	a cafeteria. *It's the quick way to say, "cafeteria".*
au bistro.	a diner. *You'll find typical French fare here—not burgers and fries, but "steak frites", steak with fries.*
au fast food.	a fast food joint.
à la pizzeria.	a pizzeria.
au resto.	a restaurant. *The quick way to say, "au restaurant".*
au boui-boui.	a little eating place. *It's similar to a dive—a tiny restaurant with less than appealing décor—but usually has pretty decent food.*
Bon ap !	Enjoy your meal! *Use this instead of the standard, "Bon appétit".*

OOPS!

After a long morning of sightseeing, two young tourists visited a village café for lunch. One tried to order some water, "de l'eau pour deux", water for two. But he mispronounced "deux" and said, "de l'eau pour Dieu", water for God. The waiter thought he was such a jackass!

dining in

Tu as pris le petit dej / un goûter*?
Did you have breakfast / a snack?
*It's French tradition for kids to break in the afternoon for a light snack.

On se fait une bouffe.
Let's have a bite. (Literally: Let's have food.)

C'est...	It's...
délicieux.	delicious.
super bon.	super good.
infect.	gross.
dégueulasse.	disgusting.
infâme.	vile.

TIP

FRENCH ETIQUETTE: MIND YOUR P's AND Q's AT THE FRENCH DINNER TABLE. HERE'S HOW...

1. It's rude not to finish everything that's on your plate, so don't take more than you can chew!

2. If you're using a knife, keep the fork in your left hand and knife in your right. If you don't need a knife, hold the fork in your right hand.

3. Don't help yourself to a second serving. Wait to be offered one.

4. While you wait, put both your hands on the table, but not your elbows.

5. If you're a guy, make sure the gal sitting next to you always has wine in her glass — a woman never helps herself to wine.

6. When everyone is done eating, don't clear only your plate — pile other people's plates with yours, then take all of them to the kitchen.

special diets

There are few vegetarians in France, and health food isn't that trendy.

Je ne mange pas de viande.
I don't eat meat.

Je suis végétarien / végétalien.
I'm a vegetarian / vegan.

Le lait me donne envie de vomir.
Milk makes me want to throw up.

Je suis au régime.
I'm on a diet.

eating disorders

Tu es...	You are...
trop maigre.	too skinny.
squelettique.	a skeleton.
anorexique.	anorexic.
boulimique.	bulimic.
gros.	fat.

12. PARTYING

let's party

On fait quelque chose ce soir.
Let's hang out tonight.

On se fait...	Let's...
une soirée sympa.	have fun tonight.
un ciné / une toile.	go to the movies.
une pièce de théâtre.	go to the theater.
un concert.	go to a concert.

Quel clubeur, celui-là !
He's really club crazy!

On va...	Let's go...
en boîte.	clubbing.
à la soirée de Jean-Luc.	to Jean-Luc's party.
dans un bar.	to a bar.

Tu danses ?
Want to dance?

Je fais une petite soirée.
I'm having a small get-together.

Hier soir, on...	Last night we...
a kiffé.	had a good time.
s'est bien amusé / marré.	had fun.
s'est éclaté.	had a lot of fun. (Literally: exploded)
a fait la teuf.	partied. *"Teuf" is verlan for "fête," party.*

smoke?

Est-ce que tu fumes ?
Do you smoke?
Say it in verlan — use "mefu" instead of "fumes".

On en grille une ?
Want to have a smoke? (Literally: Do you want to grate one?)

Tu as...?

une garettci *Verlan for "cigarette".*

une garo

une nuigrav*

un clope

un peuclo *It's verlan for "clope".*

Do you have a cigarette?

SMOKING
There isn't a minimum age to buy cigarettes in France. Smoking restrictions officially apply to all public places, including bars, restaurants, healthcare facilities, schools, offices, buses, and taxis. However, smokers are not restricted in outdoor spaces and the enforcement of the smoking ban is quite lax.

FOR THOSE WHO KNOW SMOKING IS A NASTY HABIT...
– **Tu fumes ?** Do you smoke?
– **Non !** No!

*From, "nuit gravement à la santé," very dangerous for your health, the warning label on a pack of cigarettes.

drinks

Tu veux...?	Do you want...?
un apéro	an aperitif *The short form of "apéritif".*
du pinard	wine *(Literally: cheap wine)*
un coup de rouge	a glass of red wine *(Literally: a shot of red)*
un verre	a shot
un gin tonic	a gin and tonic
une vodka orange	a screwdriver
une bière	a beer

ACCEPT AN OFFER...OR NOT.

– **Je t'offre une bière?** Can I buy you a beer?
– **Oui, merci.** Yes, thanks.
or
– **Non, c'est moi qui conduit.**
No, I'm the designated driver.

TIP

GOING OUT DRINKING IN FRANCE?

Beer is always a winner — it's cheap. "Pastis", an anise-flavored alcohol, usually mixed with water, is a must-try. If you're up for something different order: "un panaché", beer with lemonade, or "un monaco", beer with grenadine. "Malibu", the coconut-flavored rum, is totally in. And, you must try candy cocktails — alcoholic drinks accented with French candy: "Shuters Carambar", "Fraise tagada", and "Schtroumpf". These sweet treats are made by dissolving flavored candy in vodka.

THE DRINKING AGE IN FRANCE IS 18...

..but it certainly isn't enforced. You might see teenagers hanging out at cafés and drinking beer, and no one is shocked. Minors can easily purchase alcohol. Perhaps because drinking isn't seen as a big deal and it is not really a problem in France, the French don't even have an expression for "binge drinking"!

bottoms up!

Ça s'arrose !
Let's celebrate! (Literally: Let's sprinkle!)

Trinquons !
Let's cheer!

À la tienne !
Cheers! (Literally: To yours!)

Tchin, tchin !
Cheers!

Je suis pompette !
I'm tipsy!

J'ai un verre dans le nez.
I've had one drink too many. (Literally: I have one drink in the nose.)

J'ai la gueule de bois.
I'm hung over. (Literally: I have a wooden head.)

Hier soir, je/j'...	Last night I...
me suis sôulé.	got drunk.
me suis bourré la gueule.	got smashed. (Literally: filled my face)
ai pris une cuite.	got wasted. (Literally: took a cooked one)

the high life

These expressions are for reference only—these drugs are illegal in France.

Tu fumes...?	Do you smoke...?
du hashich	hashish
du shit	hashish / pot *"Shit" in verlan is "techi".*
du chichon	pot
Je suis...	I am...
déchiré.	high. (Literally: torn)
défoncé.	stoned. (Literally: smashed) *Verlan: "foncedé".*
raide-def.	fucked-up. *Short for "raide-défoncé", completely stoned.*

Je ne me drogue pas.
I don't do drugs.

busted!

On m'a...	I was...
attaqué.	attacked.
battu.	beaten.
volé / raquetté.	robbed.

Fais gaffe aux...
flics. *In verlan it's "keufs".*
poulets. (Literally: chickens)

Watch out for the cops.

J'ai été arrêté.
I got arrested.

- chill out and talk about music
- turn on the télé
- movie time

13. ENTERTAIMENT

music

Get in tune—music, "la zicmu" (**verlan** for "musique") or "la zic" (short for "zicmu") is a big part of French culture.

Ce CD est...	That CD is...
parmi les dix meilleurs.	on the top ten.
cool.	cool.
énorme.	amazing. (Literally: enormous)
super.	hot.
tip-top.	the bomb.
Ce groupe...	This group...
c'est chanmé.	is so great. *It's verlan for "méchant", nasty or mean*.
c'est de la balle / bombe.	rocks. (Literally: is of the ball / bomb)
craint.	sucks.
c'est de la merde.	sucks ass.
Tu aimes...?	Do you like...?
la dance	dance music
le hip hop	hip-hop
la house	house (music)
le jazz	jazz
la pop	pop (music)
le rap	rap
le reggae	reggae
le rock	rock n' roll
la techno	techno

necessary equipment

Tu as...?	Do you have...?
un lecteur de CD	a CD player
un discman	a discman
un walkman	a walkman
un lecteur MP3	an MP3 player
un iPod™	an iPod™
des écouteurs	earphones
une chaîne	a stereo

FACT

THE MUSICFEST

If you happen to be in France on the first day of summer, walking around any city will be music to your ears. Professional musicians as well as amateurs play in city streets during "la fête de la musique", the Musicfest, to welcome the official start of summer. You can hang out in a café and listen to one group for the whole evening or enjoy a variety of performances — from rock and techno to classical and folk music.

RAP

Rap is as popular in France as it is the world over.
Some popular French rap blends American hip-hop
style with French lyrics and northern African beats —
in fact, many of France's hottest hip-hop artists are
African immigrants from the suburbs of Paris. Though
French rap music started gaining ground in the
1980s, it's only recently that it became mainstream.

tune in to tv

Tu veux mater la télé ?   Want to watch TV?
"Mater" in verlan is "téma".

Allume la télé.   Turn on the TV.

Passe-moi la télécommande.
Give me the remote.

Tu as vu le programme télé ?
Have you seen the TV listings?

Cette émission est nulle / est cool !
That show sucks / is cool!

Éteins la télé.
Turn off the TV.

Tu aimes...?	Do you like...?
les dessins animés	cartoons
les séries	dramas
les infos	the news
les jeux	game shows
la télé réalité	reality TV
les sit-coms	sitcoms
les émissions / talk-shows	talk shows

BASIC TV IN FRANCE ISN'T FREE.
In order to receive France's six basic channels, you pay an annual tax, "la redevance". Three of the six standard channels are government owned, and showcase the news, sports, cartoons, and cultural programs—you won't find reality TV here! The other channels offer a more eclectic choice of programming: soccer, recent movies, talk shows. Cable or satellite TV with hundreds of channels—national and international—is also available.

french film

Mes films préférés sont...	My favorite movies are...
les comédies.	comedies.
les policiers.	detective movies.
les drames psychologiques.	dramas.
les films étrangers.	foreign films.
les thrillers.	thrillers.
	You can also say, "les films noirs".
les psycho-thrillers.	psycho-thrillers.

Il y a des bandes annonces ?
Are there any previews?

Le film est en version originale sous-titrée ?
Does the movie have subtitles?

Le film est en v.o. ?
Does the movie have subtitles?

La séance est à quelle heure ?
When does the movie start?

TIP

THE MOVIES

In France, making movies is an art form as well as a profitable business. In fact, with all of Paris's "cinéma d'art et d'essai", art theaters, it's easier to find a great mixture of classics, international films, and blockbuster hits than anywhere else in the world. But don't worry — you can still catch the latest releases in a multiplex on the Champs-Elysées.

American and British films are usually shown in English, with French subtitles. If you see "v.o" beside the name of the movie, this means that the film is in "version originale", with French subtitles.